SPORTS SUPERSTARS

SERENA WILLIAMS

BY THOMAS K. ADAMSON

TORQUE™

BELLWETHER MEDIA·MINNEAPOLIS, MN

Torque brims with excitement perfect for thrill-seekers of all kinds. Discover daring survival skills, explore uncharted worlds, and marvel at mighty engines and extreme sports. In *Torque* books, anything can happen. Are you ready?

This edition first published in 2023 by Bellwether Media, Inc.

No part of this publication may be reproduced in whole or in part without written permission of the publisher. For information regarding permission, write to Bellwether Media, Inc., Attention: Permissions Department, 6012 Blue Circle Drive, Minnetonka, MN 55343.

Library of Congress Cataloging-in-Publication Data

Names: Adamson, Thomas K., 1970- author.
Title: Serena Williams / by Thomas K. Adamson.
Description: Minneapolis, MN : Bellwether Media, 2023. | Series: Torque. Sports superstars | Includes bibliographical references and index. | Audience: Ages 7-12 | Audience: Grades 4-6 | Summary: "Engaging images accompany information about Serena Williams. The combination of high-interest subject matter and light text is intended for students in grades 3 through 7"– Provided by publisher.
Identifiers: LCCN 2022050067 (print) | LCCN 2022050068 (ebook) | ISBN 9798886871609 (library binding) | ISBN 9798886872866 (ebook)
Subjects: LCSH: Williams, Serena, 1981–Juvenile literature. | Women tennis players–United States–Biography–Juvenile literature.
Classification: LCC GV994.W55 A73 2023 (print) | LCC GV994.W55 (ebook) | DDC 796.342092 [B]–dc23/eng/20221019
LC record available at https://lccn.loc.gov/2022050067
LC ebook record available at https://lccn.loc.gov/2022050068

Text copyright © 2023 by Bellwether Media, Inc. TORQUE and associated logos are trademarks and/or registered trademarks of Bellwether Media, Inc.

Editor: Kieran Downs   Designer: Gabriel Hilger

Printed in the United States of America, North Mankato, MN.

TABLE OF CONTENTS

RECORD GRAND SLAM WIN	4
WHO IS SERENA WILLIAMS?	6
A RISING TENNIS STAR	8
SERENA SLAM	12
A TENNIS GREAT	20
GLOSSARY	22
TO LEARN MORE	23
INDEX	24

RECORD GRAND SLAM WIN

Serena Williams smashes a booming **serve**. She is playing against her big sister, Venus, in the 2017 Australian Open. Venus moves quickly to return the serve. Serena slams a **forehand** down the line. It is out of reach. Point for Serena!

Serena goes on to win the **match**. She sets a record for the most **Grand Slam** wins for a tennis player!

VENUS

SERENA

Battle of the Sisters

Serena and Venus faced each other in nine Grand Slam finals. Serena won seven of them.

WHO IS SERENA WILLIAMS?

Serena Williams is one of the world's best tennis players. She has won more **singles** Grand Slams than any other tennis player in the modern **era**. She and her sister, Venus, won many events together over many years. They changed tennis with their powerful styles.

SERENA WILLIAMS

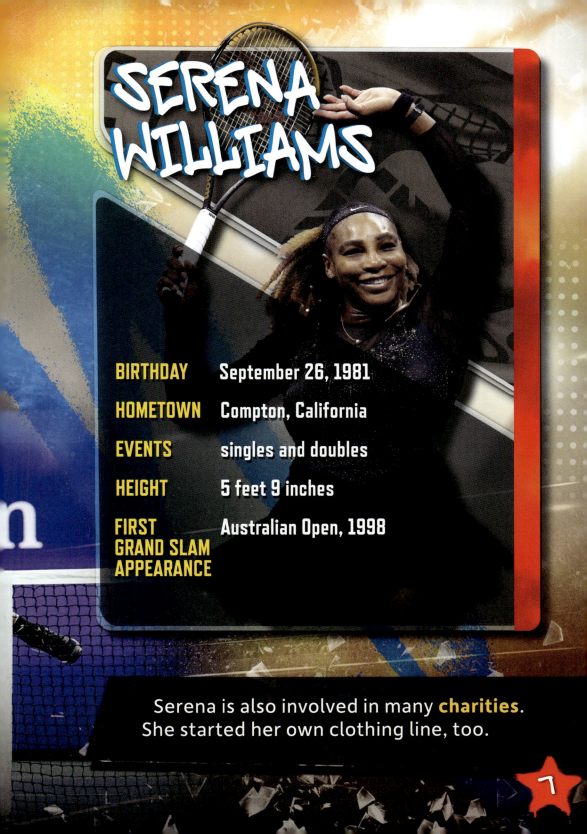

BIRTHDAY September 26, 1981

HOMETOWN Compton, California

EVENTS singles and doubles

HEIGHT 5 feet 9 inches

FIRST GRAND SLAM APPEARANCE Australian Open, 1998

Serena is also involved in many **charities**. She started her own clothing line, too.

A RISING TENNIS STAR

Both Serena and Venus were taught to play by their father, Richard. He did not know much about tennis. But he learned quickly. He kept a regular practice schedule for them.

8

In 1991, Richard decided the girls needed a **professional** coach. The family moved to Florida. The girls attended a tennis **academy**.

Williams was told not to enter pro **tournaments** until she was 16. But she did not want to wait. She entered a tournament at age 14. She lost badly.

Williams did not play as a pro again until she was 16. She began playing **doubles** with Venus in pro tournaments. This helped her gain experience.

FAVORITES

SNACK
Moon Pies

OTHER SPORT
gymnastics

AUTHOR
Maya Angelou

PET
dog

SERENA SLAM

Williams won the U.S. Open in 1999. This was her first Grand Slam win. She was only 17 years old. She and Venus also won in doubles.

The next year, they won the gold medal in doubles at the 2000 Sydney **Summer Olympics**. Serena and Venus won many more singles and doubles titles. They were gaining fans.

2000 SYDNEY SUMMER OLYMPIC GOLD MEDALISTS IN DOUBLES

Double Trouble
The Williams sisters won 14 Grand Slam doubles titles together.

From 2002 to 2003, the Williams sisters played each other in four straight Grand Slam finals. Serena won all of them. She earned her first world number 1 ranking in July 2002.

Williams had knee surgery in 2003. She won the 2005 Australian Open. But injuries forced her to miss much of the next year. In 2007, she won the Australian Open again.

In 2010, Williams had a serious problem with her lungs. She recovered, but struggled to play her best.

In 2012, she proved again she could battle back. She won Wimbledon, the U.S. Open, and an Olympic gold medal in singles that year. She also teamed up with Venus for their third doubles Olympic gold medal.

WIMBLEDON 2012

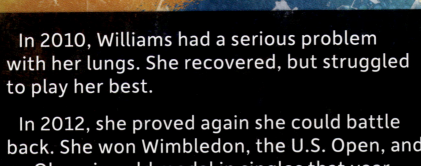

All Four

Williams has held all four Grand Slam titles at once. She called this honor the "Serena Slam." She did this twice!

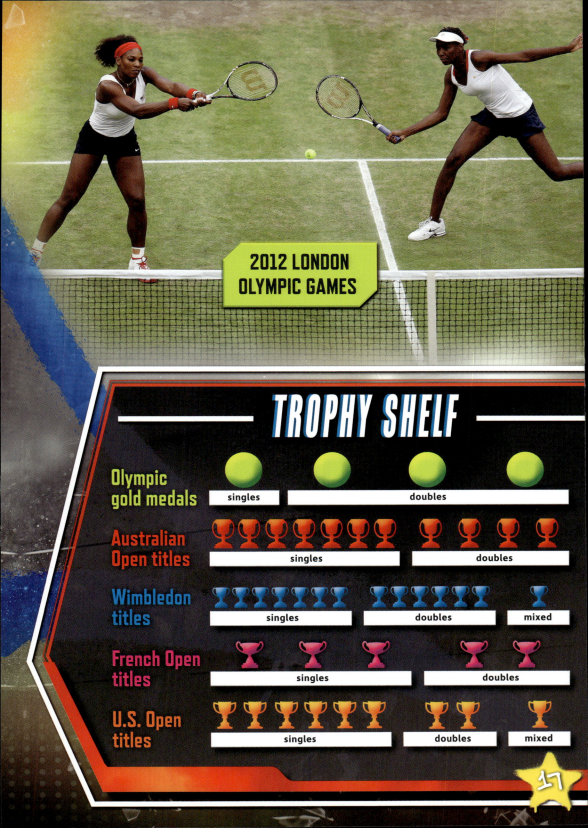

In 2017, Serena defeated Venus in the Australian Open final. It was her 23rd singles Grand Slam win.

Later that year, she gave birth to her daughter. While in the hospital, Williams had trouble breathing. She did not play tennis for a while. Then, she worked on another comeback. Over the next two years, Williams reached four more Grand Slam finals.

Record Holder

Williams became the oldest woman to win a Grand Slam when she won the 2017 Australian Open. She was 35 years, 124 days old.

TIMELINE

— June 1999 —
Williams wins her first women's doubles Grand Slam with Venus at the French Open

— September 1999 —
Williams wins her first singles Grand Slam at the U.S. Open

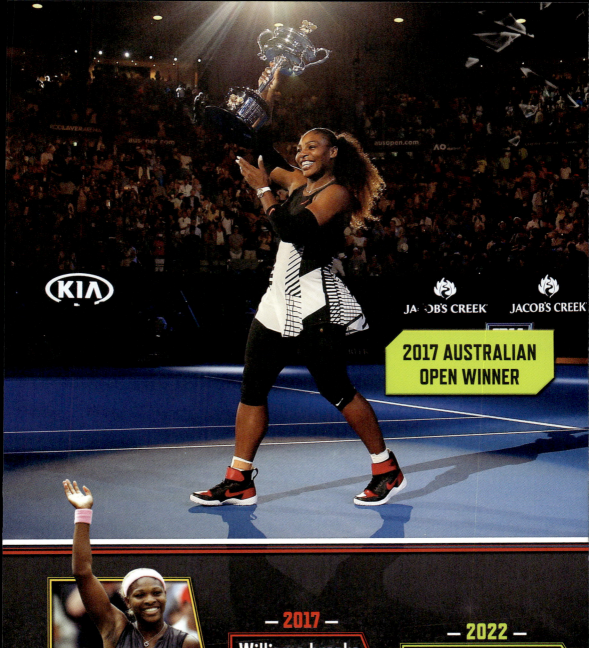

2017 AUSTRALIAN OPEN WINNER

— 2002 —
Williams is named the number 1 ranked female tennis player in the world

— 2017 —
Williams breaks the record for most Grand Slam singles titles

— 2022 —
Williams announces she will step back from tennis

A TENNIS GREAT

In 2022, Williams decided that after the U.S. Open, she would focus more on her goals outside of tennis. But she is not **retired**. She may still return to the court in the future.

Williams is more than just one of the all-time greats of tennis. She is one of history's greatest **athletes**. Her play style forever changed the game of tennis.

GLOSSARY

academy—a school that teaches a certain subject

athletes—people who are trained in or good at sports that require physical strength and skill

charities—organizations that help others in need

doubles—tennis matches with two-player teams on each side

era—a period of time in history

forehand—hitting a tennis ball on the player's dominant side

Grand Slam—one of the four most important professional tennis tournaments of the year; the Grand Slam tournaments are the Australian Open, the French Open, Wimbledon, and the U.S. Open.

match—a game between tennis players

professional—related to a player, team, or coach who makes money from a sport

retired—no longer working, or no longer playing a sport professionally

serve—the act of hitting the ball to begin play

singles—tennis matches with one player on each side

Summer Olympics—a worldwide summer sports contest held in a different country every four years

tournaments—series of matches in which players try to win championships

TO LEARN MORE!

AT THE LIBRARY

Ahrens, Niki. *Serena Williams: Tennis Superstar.* Minneapolis, Minn.: Lerner Publications, 2022.

Leslie, Jay. *Game, Set, Sisters!: The Story of Venus and Serena Williams.* New York, N.Y.: Henry Holt and Company, 2021.

Smith, Elliott. *Serena Williams.* Minneapolis, Minn.: Lerner Publications, 2020.

ON THE WEB

Factsurfer.com gives you a safe, fun way to find more information.

1. Go to www.factsurfer.com
2. Enter "Serena Williams" into the search box and click 🔍.
3. Select your book cover to see a list of related content.

INDEX

Australian Open, 4, 14, 15, 18, 19

charities, 7

childhood, 8, 9, 10, 12

doubles, 10, 12, 13, 16

favorites, 11

finals, 5, 14, 18

gold medal, 13, 16

Grand Slam, 4, 5, 6, 12, 13, 14, 16, 18

injuries, 14, 16

map, 15

match, 4, 20

profile, 7

ranking, 14

records, 4, 18

retired, 20

singles, 6, 13, 16, 18

Summer Olympics, 13, 16, 17

surgery, 14

timeline, 18–19

tournaments, 10, 20

trophy shelf, 17

U.S. Open, 12, 16, 20

Williams, Richard, 8, 9

Williams, Venus, 4, 5, 6, 8, 9, 10, 12, 13, 14, 16, 18

Wimbledon, 16

The images in this book are reproduced through the courtesy of: Leonard Zhukovsky, front cover, pp. 3, 15 (Paris, France, New York City, New York); Scott Barbour/ Stringer/ Getty Images, pp. 4, 18-19; Clive Brunskill/ Staff/ Getty Images, pp. 4-5, 14-15, 16, 17, 20-21, 23; VIEW press/ Contributor/ Getty Images, p. 6; Matthew Stockman/ Staff/ Getty Images, p. 7 (Williams); rarrarorro, p. 7 (Wimbledon flag); Paul Harris/ Contributor/ Getty Images, p. 8; Ken Levine/ Staff/ Getty Images, p. 9; Tony Marshall - EMPICS/ Contributor/ Getty Images, p. 10; picture alliance/ Contributor/ Getty Images, p. 11; Kieth Homan, p. 11 (snack); A.RICARDO, p. 11 (other sport); ZUMA Press Inc/ Alamy, p. 11 (author); Tim Clayton - Corbis/ Contributor/ Getty Images, p. 11 (pet); Carol Newsom/ Staff/ Getty Images, p. 12; Gary M. Prior/ Staff/ Getty Images, p. 13; William West/ Staff/ Getty Images, p. 15; Mo Wu, p. 15 (Melbourne, Australia); Neil Mitchell, p. 15 (London, England); Professional Sport/ Contributor/ Getty Images, p. 18 (September 1999); Bongarts/ Staff/ Getty Images, p. 19 (2002); Jean Catuffe/ Contributor/ Getty Images, p. 20.